The Landing Zone

This book has helped many people who find themselves frozen in place after losing their employment, with techniques to help them re-engage both mentally and physically in finding new opportunities for themselves and also to be better prepared for future events.

The Landing Zone

Welcome to the Mobile Workforce.

Understanding the strategies of the mobile workforce will help you reduce your unemployment cycles and begin the development of your career growth strategy.

A. Suppelsa

Published and Distributed in the United States by:

Sands Management Company INC.
PO Box 970099
Coconut Creek, FL 33097

Website: www.thelandingzonebook.com
email: info@thelandingzonebook.com

Editorial Supervisor: A. Suppelsa

Library of Congress Cataloging-in-Publication Data

ISBN: 978-0-98877450-0-1
Printed in the United States of America
1st edition, December 2012
2nd edition, Jan 2013
3rd edition, December 2014

To Betty-Jo, Bobbi-Jo and Anthony.

I love you to the moon and back!

Do not let your career define who you are.
The legacy left behind will determine who you were.

Table of Contents

Introduction

Regardless of what the economy looks like, it is imperative that you prepare as many tools and strategies to survive future employment cycles. There are hundreds of thousands of people competing for the same positions, companies and careers. The way you are going to differentiate yourself, is by having a good Landing Zone Strategy in place. This book will teach you how to by-pass the shortcomings of people who are not part of the mobile workforce and it will provide you with the strategies to guide you to have a solid plan in place. You will be able to adjust while the work force continually changes landscape.

This book will help you get both physically and mentally prepared for any transitional periods. More importantly, it will change your perspective. By being prepared ahead of time you will have the skills and the confidence to get the job done, as you have already done your homework. The best way to succeed is to learn from someone else's mistakes thereby avoiding them all together.

For example; a senior manager that was working for a top 500 company learned the hard way on how imperative it is to have a landing zone backup plan. After working his way up the corporate ladder through several promotions, he was eventually offered a severance from the company without warning. Previously thinking this could never happen to him he had a profound realization.

Over the years misguided personal thinking created a continual mental trap for not being prepared for this event to occur.

These are some examples of factors that can impede your preparedness:
1) Being a highly skilled individual and consistently ranked in the top 10% of the company.
2) Highly dedicated and giving the company the primary focus of your life, tons of overtime, late nights and weekends working.
3) Hundreds of thousands of miles traveled each year presenting and attending company meetings away from your family.
4) Dozens of patents which earned the company hundreds of millions of dollars in product revenues consumed all of your bandwidth and created an indirect consequence of being inadequately prepared.

Needless to say, it is a wakeup call that no one is untouchable for any reason or circumstance at some point having your job impacted happens to everyone.

It was during this time as an in-transition worker attempting to locate new employment that we began to better understand the new reality of the mobile workforce.

Many of the tools shared in this book are tools that were discerned during the transition period following our experiences. We hope it will change your perspective looking forward. As long as companies continue to use their workforce as a means to meet their expected profit margin gaps through workforce reductions, you will need this book to use as a reference guide for planning your future landing zone opportunities.

By being prepared ahead of time you will have the skills and the confidence to execute your plan when required, as you will have already done your homework and be ready to hit the ground running!

Chapter One

The Mobile Workforce

If you are currently employed, typically staying in a job only 28 to 36 months, have a quest for knowledge, learning and being challenged to constantly retool your skillsets, then this book is not for you. You are already part of the Mobile Workforce. If you are not in that position this book is for you. You will be ahead of the curve. This book will teach you the understanding of how the new model works and how employers are changing their strategies, product development and innovation cycles around this new workforce model. Once you are part of the mobile workforce, and understand the warning signs you will know when to move from understanding the key indicators of when it is time to make a career change.

The days of discovering companies that you can spend an entire career from entry level to retirement, are gone. This is why the mobile workforce exists. Those approaching 30 years or younger understand it and have mastered the art of continually scoping out and seeking what is next. They are aware of their landing zones areas. This translates into future job opportunities and ultimately career development. Rest assured after reading this book you too will know how to develop your own landing zone areas.

Understanding what the difference is between a job and a career is essential.

A job is something that allows you pay all of your bills on time every month. If you cannot pay your bills on time every month, then you need to focus on improving your skills and changing your career into a higher income potential area. You could love your job and feel passionate about what you are doing at work. If you are not advancing at work in pay, growth in levels or experiences, it is not a career but a job. If you are in this situation you will be lucky to be able to keep up with inflation overtime.

A career is the desire to do whatever it takes to get to the next level, and increase your income or social status. For a career, you have to be able to pick up and move yourself and your family at a moment's notice as the next opportunity presents itself in order to advance to the next level inside or outside of the company. Hence the mobile workforce exists.

If you are currently not focused on this, then you are currently working in a job. This is not where you want to be. When you are working in the job category gravity is always pulling you backwards from learning new skills. As time goes on your skills become obsolete. Technology is transforming and before you know it, you find yourself out of a job. Cost reductions, organizational changes, sector losing money; you were living in the wrong state or for whatever the reason, you are now out of a job.

This transformation to defeat gravity on skill development is driving young people to abandon their existing employers early because they are not being challenged enough in their job or they are not learning enough competitive skills. This creates the mobile workforce. Talented people are on the quests for further skill development, challenges and are looking for employers to increase their skillsets. If you are not part of the Mobile Workforce currently, at some point you will be forced into to this new ecosystem of survival.

Chapter Two

Be Prepared

At some point in your life whether you are a high or low potential person, you are going to get caught up in a downsizing, layoff, separation or termination event. When it occurs you are going to either hit the ground running after that next opportunity, or you are going to be spending one to two months with a career management company who are patting you on the back making you feel good about yourself. They are going to be helping you prepare your resume, and training you on the interviewing process. Depending on the level of position you held previously the extent of the patting on the back will vary from none, to six months maybe even a year. Let's face facts, most companies hire career management companies to help severed employees go through the transitional process to finding a new job. But their primary focus is to keep impacted candidates busy so they will keep their minds off of litigation opportunities beyond the 49 day revocation period of the signing of the company release documentation. Within the management company you can cry in their office about how you loved your previous job, how things are not fair and they will pat you on the back and tell you everything is going to be alright. What they are not telling you is that once you have lost your current job, all of your leverage is gone, whether you realize it or not. This process of taking an impacted person and transforming and training them to go out and get another job can take in upwards of four to six weeks, maybe even longer.

If you are not prepared you will need the help of a transitional management services company and you will be blessed if you ever get this opportunity to work with one since their services can only be acquired through the severing company and not on an individual basis.

So the lesson here is if you are not prepared for this to happen to you, you need to understand and start the transformation process now before it arises so you can hit the ground running should it come to pass.

Speaking with all of the high potential people that I interviewed that were unexpectedly impacted in their career, the fastest any one single person could obtain employment into another company was two months and the longest was 18 months. This variance was also dependent on the company size. The smaller the company, the faster you could get in the door, but the expected salaries were also smaller. If you are a salaried person of $150K or more you can expect to wait up to one month for every $10K of salary or up to 15 months if you wanted to enter employment at or above your previous level. In most cases, the time to obtain a better position than you previously held was even longer than the 15 months, so you must be prepared to be able to wait out the storm. This way you are not going to be forced into accepting a lower level position earning less than you are accustomed to receiving.

Here is an example of an authentic best case scenario. Downsizing was occurring at a high tech company. It impacted over 100 people in a single department. A competing company, located seven miles down the road had about 200 open requisitions looking for high tech people. Knowing this, the manager called over to the other company and told his friend that he had one particular person that had key skills that he knew they were looking for within the other company. Even with an open requisition from the time the person left the original company, it took six to eight weeks before he started at the new company. The interviewing process consisted of multiple visits, offer negotiations, acceptance procedures, background checks and drug testing. This increased the transition time line from one company to another from weeks to months.

On occasion, you can land an opportunity in a couple of weeks. If it does happen, that is fantastic and you can accumulate all of your severance pay if you received a severance package. If you are able to bank your severance, make sure to put it away in your reserves fund to expand your duration time if required for future use.

As the length of unemployment duration goes on for longer than expected. The mental strain increases due to the negative effects of the cash flow equation being depleted without being replenished. This stress is normal. The stress level may drive you to take a position that is a lower level and for less pay if your funds are significantly being depleted. The determination of whether or not you are going to survive this event is based on one thing and one thing only. Have you saved enough money in your reserves to ride out your period of unemployment? If your company gives you a severance package, it helps this situation, but I would not count on this as the only life line.

BUDGET, if you do not know how to budget now is the time to learn.

How do you determine the appropriate amount of funds required to ride out your storm? First of all everyone is different based on their position, wages and skill level. From the best case scenario of people interviewed you would need a minimum of eight weeks of expenses saved up in reserves. In the worst case scenario you will need a minimum of one month for every $10K of your salary. In most cases, the relatively safe number is six months, with the added benefit of controlled spending during the duration of your unemployment.

Forcing strict control on spending could extend out your savings to a longer period of time. If you are impacted, try not to spend money on things that are not basic necessities. The goal is to make your financial reserves last as long as possible. That way you will have the leverage to negotiate when an offer arrives.

Calculate the total expense number you need to establish 100% of what you spend every month. If the total monthly budget spend totals $7,600 a month, then you should have access to a minimum of $45,600 or a cash equivalent account. When a person is impacted it takes them time to stop spending the way they are accustomed to living, estimating with the total spend amount each month is extremely insightful. It is especially beneficial to set aside these funds, so you do not have to take money out of your 401K or conventional retirement accounts. If you do not already have your reserve accounts setup then start one today. If you are not able to save the funds to grow your account then you should seek financial counseling to help you determine a budget that you can live within your means.

The Resume and Cover Letter are the second most valuable thing to have completed after you have established your security fund levels. Everyone should have a polished resume and cover letter ready to go at a moment's notice. The mobile workforce has one in a polished form and so should you. Even once they attain a new job it is likely within the first year of service those individuals are already searching for their future opportunities. This is why the resume and cover letter are so critical. If you do not have one ready and lost your job you could waste several weeks putting one together. Secondly, if you do not have a solid cover letter and resume it will not make it past the resume screeners. The resume screeners are the people that are helping the hiring manager look for qualified candidates. They are not necessarily technical, but they are looking for key words. If you submit for a position at a company without a cover letter they will cast the resume aside as a sign of the submitter's laziness. A polished resume and cover letter ready to go at all times will give you an edge and allow you to be looking for your next opportunity without wasting valuable time in your job search.

If you have a resume and it is not polished in a perfect format and you are thinking of sending it out for on-line postings or emailing it to an employer for employment opportunities, STOP!!! Do not do it! If you submit a resume for a posting and it was reviewed and rejected for the position, you will never be able to reapply for that position again. You will be listed in their database for the posting as having already been screened and rejected for that position. This position might have been a perfect fit, the dream job you wanted, a higher level position than you previously held but you missed it. That is why the presentation of who you are and what you are trying to achieve has to be in excellent condition. You might only have a single opportunity to earn approval through the screening system and enter into the interviewing process. Keeping an up to date resume and various cover letters formats are vital to your long term career success story. If you do not know how to accomplish this on your own find an executive management class / organization and learn how to write a formal formatted resume and various cover letters. Keeping it up to date should be part of your ongoing career management practice. If you are not managing your career, no one else is going to be doing this for you. You have to be proactive.

The only value you have to a company is your ability to leave and work for another company. This might seem counter intuitive, but when other companies want you to work for them, you are in demand. When you are in demand your value increases and how much you earn can go up substantially. Finally, the core skills that you already have obtained can provide value to another company or industry. Make sure your resume and cover letter includes how they relate to the market place. Determining and knowing how these skills work together in different areas can create unique and different opportunities. These opportunities are what I refer to as landing zones. It is essential to understand and realize your landing zone areas and how to prepare to use them when the time requires.

Chapter Three

The Warning Signs

The mobile workforce has low service club time with a company. Likely if a reduction of force occurs they would be getting the smallest severance packages, ranging from 2 to 8 weeks of severance pay. Knowing the signs of when it is time to move on is extremely critical. It is easier to land a new job while you currently have one. Being proactive is essential to survival.

There are two types of warning signs; one that tells you it is time to look for another career at another company and one that is a key indicator that you are currently in the radar for losing your current position.

The best leverage you have to find a new job at another company is while you are still working. Looking for your next opportunity while you still have an employer is the best scenario. Once you are not currently employed you have lost your leverage. You will be looking for a job to replace your existing salary and the choices will be dependent on your skill sets, your willingness to relocate and your predetermined landing zones. The best thing to do is not ignore the warning signs and start looking for opportunities as they present themselves.

Signs of when it is time to seek changing companies.

1) **The company posts a negative quarter**. This will most likely lead to economic restrictions, downsizing or cut backs. If you have any specialized talents this is the time to move to a company that is growing and exciting. If you do not have any key talent the less chance you have to move. Therefor you need to be working on expanding your network contacts for opportunities.

2) **The company is for sale, or being positioned to be sold**. Once the company is bought the new administration will come in and start cutting, changing out the management structure and reorganizing. Most takeovers or acquisitions are of companies that are in trouble. Caution: if you are a mid to high level manager, most likely you will be the first one to go with the transition.

3) **You are no longer learning any new skills** and your employer does not provide training or tuition reimbursement programs within the company, your company is continually scaling back its employee benefits without adding other ones to attract new talent.

4) If your manager's goal was for you to replace them and at some point, that **plan is no longer being acted on**; it is time to move on.

5) The company is 100% controlled by decisions made from Finance and Human Resources organizations and is **not focused on innovation**.

6) The company implements or has standardized ranking and rating systems as the only vehicle for work force reduction.

Individual Warning Signs:

1) **You are in the top 10%** of the company ranking and rating system and you do not receive stock options while others above you and below you receive them. This is a high level sign that you are no longer seen as critical talent. It's time to start networking for that next position.

2) If **your budget is getting reduced**, it may be an early sign that things are going south. Having to do more with less are possible indications of downsizing.

3) Another sign is if your manager tells you indirectly, that at some point in the near future you will **have to move to the headquarter location**. Perhaps you are working at the wrong location and they want you to move without a move package without financial assistance. If that is the case the company is reorganizing. They have determined key sites and non-key sites, and you maybe currently are located at a non-key site. They are not willing to disclose this information to you. It is time to move on. Do not ignore the warning signs.

4) If the company **severance package is being reduced** overtime, do not to wait around for the payout. Move to a new opportunity while you still have your leverage from your existing position.

Many times there are signs, indicators, or internal voices that occur telling us there might be a problem. Often times we do not want to acknowledge them because we perceive things as going well. Why mess with a good thing? Many times looking backwards you are able to see them clearly. After you have been through the cycle a single time you will be able to see them right away. Learn to look for them upfront and take action if required.

Unconsciously you might find or catch yourself searching for jobs through the internet. It might be because you are curious, it is a slow time at work or you are bored currently with what you are doing. Are these signs of your unconscious telling you it is time to move on? What is causing this? Is your driving passion no longer being met? Without you even knowing it your subconscious is trying to drive you towards something new and exciting. "What do you think it is trying to tell you?"

When you are passionate about what you are doing, many times you do not even think about eating or taking a break let along having time to cruise the internet. Unless your passion is for searching itself, this maybe a sign that you are starting to lose, or have lost your passion altogether for what you are currently doing. Most people enjoy working the most at what they are most passionate about. Do you know what your passion is? If not, then go out there and find it!

Many times multiple calls and email inquiries from recruiters often times might be a sign that something is going on or about to happen. Recruiters want to get to you prior to you going to a company website and apply for a position around them. If they find you after you have already submitted your resume they cannot collect on you because you are already in the system.

If you are in demand as a resource you will get a ping inquiry from a recruiter about once every one to two weeks. When all of a sudden you are getting two to three inquires a week you will know something is up. Often times they know your company is going to be downsizing before you know what is going on. How you might ask? Many times a state requires a company to file a notice to the state if reductions are going to be occurring at that company. Monitor the compliance boards and you will be able to know what is going on ahead of time.

A good practice when you get inquiries from recruiters is put them in touch with people from your network that need that connection if you do not need that opportunity yourself. It helps the people in your network find a connection and the recruiter also will be able to capitalize on finding someone quickly if they can close the deal.

Many times the warning signs are there and often times are easier to ignore them then to act on them. This is the number one failure mode for people that have been in a position for a very long time. Ultimately it comes down to being afraid of change itself! It is easier to go with what you know and what you know how to do already. Living off of your own memory map is easy. Staying on your preprogrammed map long-term equates to lower stress and an easier life with less variability.

"It was like a warm blanket that I just did not want to take off a person had once said to me as to why they had stayed at the company for so long."

No Change for a very longtime translates into being very comfortable. You would think if you changed jobs every two to three years people would view you as not being able to hold down a job! On the other hand if you worked at a company for 20 years their view of the person would be of lacking drive or being complacent. Question: "Why again did you stay at that company so long?" Many times the person, who cannot hold a position, gets picked for a position over a long term employee because they are viewed as having more experience than the person who stayed at the same company for 20 years. In many cases instead of looking for a dedicated employee they are looking to benefit from the experiences from the combined mobile workforce experiences. Be prepared to know the signs and how you will respond ahead of time is the key to your long term career success.

Chapter Four

The Landing Zone Strategy – Hindsight is 20/20

Over the course of your career, you are changing roles and responsibilities learning new skills and whether you know it or not you are creating landing zone opportunities. The problem with most people is they do not know how to determine the landing zones. They may not know how to prepare to use them if required. Most people are fixated on an onward and upward direction inside their existing company. If that individual was impacted they would continue to visualize their previous existing career path. In their mind as if it is still there. But in reality it is gone. The single largest mistake of an impacted person, besides not being prepared financially, is being fixated on trying to replace the career they previously had and not looking forward at all possible opportunities.

When Cortez came to the new world, he burned his ships in the harbor to send a signal to his crew that they were not returning to the Old World as they knew it, and it was the New World he wanted them to focus on. Once you have lost your existing career follow as Cortez did and get rid of the old career path and prepare to create a new plan. "Your primary job now is to find a new career". Keep the same schedule, get up and follow the same routine as you did before, but instead of working for your former employer, you are working for yourself. You can create a new career path with a new or existing company if you start from a landing zone opportunity.

Impacted you have lost your leverage. There is no demand for companies to offer you more unless they were asking you to come out of retirement or they genuinely wanted you and you were in the capacity to hold out of the workforce for a long duration. As stated previously with proper planning you will have the financial reserves behind you, so you do not have the pressure on you to cave in for the low ball offer.

Finding a landing zone position is entirely based on planning ahead of time. That along with previously developed skillsets you now have the ability to fit into different areas. For this example, I am showing a career path of a person who stayed at a single employer for an exceedingly long time. When you first start your career at an Entry Level position you were fresh out of school with perhaps one to two years of experience you encompassed learning new skills and processes that were required to perform the job. Progress over time watched you grow into a Project Manager, Program Manager, Manager, Senior Manager, Director and then to VP of the company, and maybe even President. At each of these levels, there were certain barriers to overcome and new skillsets that had to be learned. The single largest mishap that commonly occurs with most people in their career path is that over the course of these movements, they do not know how each of the levels obtained was connected to other industries and what job requirements were needed to support these positions at determined levels within those industries.

For instance, a Project Manager in the tech industry working on cell phone designs would have been able to obtain their PMP certification through on the job training with their company. The PMP certification spans as a requirement for all project managers across various industries. The product certification process across industries is vastly different. Product certification differences between tech and medical are distinctly different. Just having the PMP certification is not enough to allow a person to easily jump between industries. What comes into play is knowing the specific product certification process. While the person was in the Tech industry learning the FCC acceptance and other processing criteria they could have also taken training courses on the FDA validation, 510K and PMA certification, or submission process and requirements that would have created a landing zone opportunity for them to slide from the Tech industry to the Medical device industry more readily.

It is important not to be totally immersed in a particular career path or industry, and to be looking around at the other adjacent industries areas to obtain more diversified Landing Zone opportunities.

Every person needs to ask themselves, what skillsets am I missing to be able to work in adjacent industries. They need to look at the skillsets that are common between industries and determine what skillsets they need to develop that are of value. Determine the missing areas, then you must immediately seek training, so the Landing Zone opportunity is confirmed for future use.

Landing Zones are pre-identified based on existing jobs skills matched to a job in a particular industry. These positions might be a position you had held previously. In some cases, a landing zone position might pay 10% to 30% less than you are used to currently making. Don't be appalled by the thought of going backwards. If you look at the total cash equation you are limiting your losses by generating some income, while continuing to look for opportunities to present themselves within the existing company as well as looking at other companies. The most significant aspect of finding a Landing Zone opportunity is having your leverage back for future negotiations. Landing Zone opportunities are not designed to replace your past career, but rather a place to create or start a new career from.

The Mobile Workforce does not have this problem because they jump between industries. They might have started in tech entry level and then jumped over to a medical device entry level position and therefore now learned all of the process steps, acceptance criteria and procedures for both industries, thus creating a larger skill base. The mobile Workforce is working for themselves and not for the benefit of a company. The sooner you adopt this mentality the better off you will be. From here on out, you are working for yourself!

Continuously building and retooling your skills should become part of your typical day to day routine. A good practice to adopt is too always making it a point to study pertinent information for one hour a day. Your goal should be to try to learn at least one new thing each day. Your mindset should be that of a lifelong learner. Don't sell yourself short by ending your learning after earning your degree. The degree is only the beginning of the lifelong learning journey. Lifelong learning is required to maintain competitiveness.

Without updating your skills, gravity is always pulling you backwards and soon you will be outdated.

Make it a point to continually invest in yourself. If you find that you are looking for work for more than sixty days without getting any callbacks you need to think about looking at your current skillsets and seek some current training to get traction on your search effort.

Part of the work force rehabilitation programs offered scholarships for skill development. Through these programs you can get free training in PMP project management, network management, web page designs, online application programming and Six Sigma training to make you more competitive in the workplace. All of these programs are more accessible if you were part of a Warren Act work force reduction in force, versus not.

Take all of the free training that you can get exposed to that interests you and could allow you to create another landing zone area. Can you think of training that you are interested in or something you always wanted to try? Now is the time to go after it instead of being idle, you having nothing to lose in learning something new! Every degree or certification you get is only the beginning of the life time learning cycle.

Chapter Five

Focus on the Job or Career you want!

After spending time working it will not take you long to determine what you like and do not like about a particular job or career. If you love what you do and cannot get enough of it each day, then stick with what you are doing. If you do not love what you are currently doing then it is time to seek change. The only way to be long-term successful is to love your work as if it were a breath of fresh air.

Money on its own is not a long term satisfier. It is enjoyable, more is better; but it is not 100% of the equation. Positive and negative effects can make or break a person's outlook and long-term individual success. Loving what you do is what brings out the fire and passion that creates the positive energy in the workplace and will make you successful long-term.

Each time you have the opportunity to change jobs or careers it is essential to visualize the job or career you would like to have. See yourself driving to work, interacting with the people, and truly loving it. If you are going to envision a company to work for, make it is one that you love. Create it as a mental picture, and stay focused on what you are trying to accomplish. Make sure to stay away from the negative thoughts and images, as well as people who are negative and condescending. All of these things will prevent you from pursuing your dream job.

If you know what you want to obtain, write it down and develop a plan. Be as specific as possible. The importance of writing it down is that you will be able to have it as a reference. You can refer back to as your career search changes and grows.

If you know you want to work for XYZ Company, write it down. I want to work for XYZ Company making $XXX every year. Review this information daily and each day write down one thing that you did that day that got you closer to your goal. Maintained focus is what helps obtain the goal in the end.

Never give up on what you want.
Perseverance equals success!

While manifesting your new career it is necessary to remember the job search is not only about sitting in front of the computer 20 hours a day searching job boards. It is especially pertinent to make sure you take time to exercise and remain physically and mentally fit. Keep a balanced life, eat right and exercise. Know who you are, and love yourself. Being comfortable with yourself exudes confidence and interviewers will see that in your presence.

No one will want to hire you if you are not willing to hire yourself first. Market and create a showcase about yourself depicting all aspects of your life. You are going to have to decide up front, if the opportunity is going to come to you, or are you going to find the opportunity. Make sure to get out there and meet the people who have the same interests as you have in other areas outside of your immediate industry focused area.

*An acronym to remember is to get **FIT**.
(**Fitness, Intelligence and Tenacity**)*

Fitness is crucial because people want to hire people who look and feel successful. There is nothing more self-confident than saying "Hey, look at me!" **Intelligence** is being a lifelong learner. Successful managers want to be surrounded by intelligent people to help make themselves and the organization successful. Thus creating demand for intelligent people. **Tenacity** is continually having the ability to showcase your intrinsic worth without giving up on your dreams of what you want to accomplish.

At the end of the day when all is said and done, what your intrinsic value to the company is what differentiates you from other people in the population.

When the dream opportunity shows up you will be ready to impress the hiring manager with the whole package that you have developed. The people who think they can be successful are usually the ones that are successful! The hiring managers want to surround themselves with people who want to be successful and have the self-confidence and right skill sets to get the job done. The key is to be that person.

Chapter Six

Proper Networking and finding the jobs that are not posted.

If you are looking for a position that has an income of $140K a year or more you are not going to find it posted on the internet. If you see a job posted for greater than this amount or higher on the internet it maybe because the company is trying to meet fair recruiting practices. Often times they already know the person they want to hire but post the positon on the internet anyway. Through having a large number of people apply for posted positions, they review them and reject them to meet their fair recruiting requirements. A company may even bring you in to an interview for the sole purpose of satisfying these internal requirements. They need to make sure the correct number of people were interviewed to satisfy their due diligence criteria. Unless you are a physician, the chance of getting a response from an online posting with an income greater than $140K a year is very low. Positions of these high financial levels are usually handled by executive recruiter looking to find a specific person and not the other way around.

The best place to find jobs for less than $140K per year is through internet postings from RECRUITERS.

There is an entire industry of people whose sole purpose in life is to search for qualified talent. They are called recruiters. Recruiters can make 30% plus of the starting salary of a placed employee if the high level placed employee stays in their position for more than six months or other specified time. In order to get the high-end career advancement and find jobs that have the enormous salaries, benefits and perks you have to find the right recruiters. Sometimes recruiters will seek you out for specific skills, capabilities and talents.

It is great to be in this position, but for most people you need to make a plan on how to find the recruiters that work within your network of opportunities. Unless it is a retained search from the company the recruiter only gets paid when they place the person inside of the company.

Companies that are looking for key talent seek out the help of recruiters. Recruiters represent companies in search of specific talent, but once a recruiter establishes a connection with a candidate that they have placed that has earned them high revenues even if that person eventually leaves the company they most likely will not look to place that same person into another company again. Typically a single agency will only place an individual a single time.

The best way to find a new job is to find out which jobs are not posted yet. The best way to do this is to expand your recruiter network and personal network into other companies. In most cases, the person that gets the job is known by someone within the hiring company. Frequently you hear at work "Do you know anyone that might know how to do this specific function", and you say, "Hey I know someone" and the next thing you know they are working at the company. Sometimes you see a posting online and you apply for it on-line with help of someone from your network. You then contact that person to submit a copy of your resume to the hiring manager with a personal recommendation. This is called using the runner. It is actually the number one way to get a position within a company.

Get into your **C.A.R.** (**C**ontacts, **A**ware, and **R**unner) and drive yourself to your next opportunity. "**C**" is for the **contacts** that you already know in your network. The "**A**" contacts are the people "**aware**" of an opportunity or jobs that are going to come available in the near future or are currently available. The "**R**" contacts are the people that are going to be "**running**" your resume to the hiring manager. In some regard, the A people might be also considered as the bridge people in your network. In most cases they may know of someone or heard of someone with an opportunity. The A people have discussions with the C people through casual conversation. Through this exchange the information gets back to you. If interested the **C** connection contacts their **A** connection and the **A** connection places the **R** connection.

The key is to determine how to connect the opportunity to the runner. In order to get anywhere you need to have a **CAR** path that is well defined. It is tremendously relevant to expand your personal network. While you are growing it try to focus on the

CAR strategy you are going to want to drive towards your success story.

Even with finding that next opportunity you will need to grow your network, to find the "**A**" who know the "**R**" people. So remember **C** = Current Connections, **A** = People Aware of an Opportunity, and **R** = The person running your resume to the hiring manager with a recommendation. In some cases, the **C, A** and the **R**, or the **A** and the **R** could be the same person. In most cases you find opportunities from the people that you already have in your network. Of all of the people I interviewed, the ones who found opportunities the fastest, used the runner approach to get to the hiring manager. "It is all about the people who you know" is such a true statement.

You can never have too many connections. The key is to find people who are **AWARE** of an opportunity. This may occur through casual conversation with people or conversation that occurs with your connections. You need to communicate your needs in order to promote awareness of what position you are looking whenever you are having casual conversations with others in your current network connections. Be remarkably specific. Prepare for those conversations ahead of time.

I call this a planned, spontaneous conversation. For the person receiving the information, it seems to them an impromptu conversation. However in fact it is planned and rehearsed ahead of time and stored in the memory bank until it is needed to be used. When you communicate your needs out to your contacts, a connection is possibly made by one of them who may be aware of an opportunity or someone in their own contacts is aware of an opportunity. You may or may not know the actual person who is aware of the opportunity, but the connection is made. If someone tells you of a person who is aware of an opportunity it is imperative for you to **follow-up** to make the connection with this person and get the information. The most relevant information to get from the person besides the job information is the name of the HIRING MANAGER. You can also ask: "do they know anyone who knows that person." Hence you are able to identify the RUNNER individual. The runner individual is the person who is going to be running your resume to the hiring manager. If you are not able to connect with the RUNNER then ask the person who gave you the contact information to ask the person to run the resume to the hiring manager for you.

If you are considering going to your networking resources to start sending invitations to connect to high level contacts at various companies, my suggestion is not to do it. Building out your network is going to take some time and effort. If you bypass this process and try to connect with a high level person and they do not know you and you interview with the company, the person is going to be thinking, here is the person that tried to connect with me and I do not know them, so right off of the bat you are on the wrong foot at the start of the interview. The moral of the story is: if you do not know the people do not try to connect with them unless you have had a conversation with them, or you have been introduced, if you worked at the same company previously, or you are part of the same professional networking group. If it does not fall into one of these four areas and you try to connect, you could be burning your bridges without even knowing it.

If you currently have no connections, focus on finding recruiters in your industry. High Volume Recruiter's (HVR) post online jobs opportunities in their on line network. If you are part of their network you will be able to view the opportunities as they are posting online. Here in lies the problem. Recruiters are hired by companies and are not here to work for or place individuals. Yes, they have an interest of expanding their network since you might know someone they could place in a position which would earn them revenue. If you find a job posting or hear of a job, the first thing you should try to determine is who is the recruiter for this position, and then try to connect into them. Instead of them searching, the search comes to them. Think of it as finding a job in reverse, or reverse engineering a job.

High Volume Recruiters publish their jobs on the internet. Like trolling for fish, hoping to connect with someone who is a candidate or knows a candidate that can generate them revenue. Find the HVR's that are of interest to you by the types of jobs they publish and stay connected to them within your network. If you are able to help them with some candidate leads then they will be more willing to help you with networking through their other connections. This may lead to other placement opportunities that they know about from their other recruiter network. The Mobile

Workforce are always monitoring these daily postings for their next career move.

Recruiters can help you make strategic connections with people from their network. One time I helped a recruiter with multiple placements at a single company on an urgent need from people that I had known in my network. Turning down the referral fee, this person in return knew I was trying to build out my network. They called a high level person at a local company that I was trying to break into and got me connected with a personal friend for a networking connection. The message from the recruiter was "Hello John (SVP) for years we have worked together recruiting talent. There is an exceptionally good friend of mine who has some skillsets that there might be of future value in you networking together if the opportunity presents itself." The best part of this connection is once the SVP knows you; they might be having a conversation with a C-level person from another company who is looking for a specific talent. This person would remember that you were out there and therefore you may be tipped off to a job that is being created before it has been posted.

My suggestion is to list out the top 50 companies you would like to work for in the future by location. Work on establishing connections in all of the companies through people you have had conversations with. Introductions from known people, and people who are in common groups you attend. You might be thinking 50 companies is a large number, but if your desire is stay in a particular area and not have to relocate, 50 companies might be low if you have niche talent or expertise. Companies are constantly going thru cycles of changes. You need to make sure these cycles are available at the same time you are looking for a new position. Make sure they are companies across all landing zone areas.

It is imperative you ensure you are connected to the human resource talent acquisition person from each of the companies you are targeting. The talent acquisition person will post their positions online and being connected to them, will give you information to be able to determine which companies are hiring and which one are not. Often times it is the talent acquisition person that is going to the recruiter to find a candidate. If they initially tried to find a candidate and were not successful, they expand their search with the recruiter and their expanded network. If you want to beat out the recruiters, know the talent acquisition people well. I mean extremely well!

Another way to obtain fabulous networking connections is to do volunteer work. Large companies are leaning towards helping the community and giving back. Believe it or not, if you ever attended a popular volunteer event you would not be surprised to find a lot of high level people are in there donating their time from different companies. Once you have met them and said hello, have a conversation, or work side by side with them, make sure to follow-up and make them part of your network. You could introduce yourself in the invitation to connect with "Hello, It was truly delightful to meet you at the volunteer event. I would like to add you to my personal network. I also hope to see you and work with you at the next event. If you know of any other events that you think I might be interested in supporting please let me know and I would be happy to volunteer for the event." Regards John Doe.

The bottom line is you need to have connections with other people in other companies if you want to find new opportunities and grow within your career. This includes finding landing zone opportunity bases to create new career paths. Each connection you make should have a defined understanding for potential career development or landing zone potential opportunities so make each connection count. I suggest mapping out your network by the company and people. So when you focus on your networking areas you are focused on specific companies that are of interest to you.

Chapter Seven

The First Call, Screening and Interview Process

In most cases, you are going to have three to five points of contact in the interviewing process. The initial call, the screening manager, first interview, second interview, and the final interview. If you had applied for an online position posted by HVR or another recruiter who was in a search for a candidate and they had pulled your resume at some point you are going to get the first call.

The first call is a screening call to determine whether or not you have the requirements to merit an interview in person. The first caller is a person screening candidates for the hiring manager. Once the screener has determined you meet the criteria they pass the information to the hiring manager and they set up a phone or online interview with you. Once the hiring manager finds you are a possible fit, he brings you in to interview with other people on his team. They do this to see if they like you enough to hire you.

This is a tremendously pertinent point in the process. The hiring manager might not even be present while you are at the company interviewing. He has already picked you and is now awaiting feedback from the other people. It is important to make sure when you are called to an interview, that you find out all of the possible people with whom you are going to interview with. Try to research everything you can about them before you go to the interview.

Download the (10K) annual report information about the company, markets, products and plans and study them to prepare for the interview day. The best preparation for an interview is to study the top 100 interview questions posted on the internet. Relate the questions to your own experiences. Research sites where people have posted their interview questions to get a sense of what questions they might be asking during your interview.

When the screener or recruiter is interested in bringing you in for an interview, even though you would not take the position, go anyway! The experience of the interviewing process for training is invaluable. It could also get you some new networking connections. You will also learn additional information on current salary scales for the market. This rule is the same for networking meetings. When in doubt always go. Dress in proper business attire. First impressions are extremely important!

Never engage in a salary expectation too early in the interviewing process. Make them want you first before any terms are negotiated. If the interviewer needs to have a salary amount give them a range.

You do not want to close the door on an interview just because they think your salary requirement is higher than they can afford. Be Flexible!

During the interviewing process you are going to have anywhere from one to four interviews during the hiring process. The higher level you are the more repeat interviews you are likely to have occur. Usually a single interview could run from a couple of hours to all day. If they ask you back it may mean they are interested in you and they want to expose you to more of their staff, at some point. The more you return for repeat interviews it has a diminishing return value. The fourth interview is the magic number. On this interview you want to ask them what the next steps in the process of being hired into the company.

Sometime employers have issues with commitment of filling the position. Or they are looking for free consulting advice. At this point or at any point during the interviewing process if you do not ask for the job you will never get the position. Be sure to ask!

After four days of interviews it would be the equivalent of about $10K of free consulting advice, so make sure you know what you are worth. Be prepared to only give them half of the solutions with an added token of "if you hired me, I could help you implement these solutions". The best way to get free consulting advice is to interview high level candidates and ask them to propose solutions to your highest company problems and issues.

In actuality, the hiring managers hiring for any position have the hardest job. They need to determine if you can do the job; will you do the job, if and will you get along with the rest of the population. They have in an exceedingly short time frame in which to do this. This is why during any interview process the probability of being asked the top 100 interviewing questions is extremely high. The focus may be more than how you respond to the questions, but also composure and dynamics of how you answer the questions. Turning negative into positives, maintaining composure and focused answers are all factors that play into maintaining their work dynamic. Most of the time a hiring manager's success rate is a little over 50% of finding someone that will 100% fit into the organization. From the hiring manager's standpoint, the first time you see a candidate you are seeing their A level behavior. After a couple of months, usually 6 to 18 months in the workforce you start seeing the C, D, and F behavior.

Always send a thank you note. When they first contact you send a thank you note. When they setup an interview, send a thank you note. After an interview follow up and summarize what you talked about. Make sure to correspond with each person you interacted with during the interviewing process. When the job offers come or otherwise, always send a thank you note appreciating their time and efforts.

Part of the closure process in the job searching process is being thankful.

Through this process you will come to realize, how the agility of your network can either make or break your success story. You will find that people you had helped to find employment opportunities previously might not reciprocate the favor, or perhaps a complete stranger might go the extra mile helping you toward your next opportunity. Knowing how valuable your network is to your success, the best practice to always send a thank you note to every person you interacted with along your journey. The reason I call it a journey is it never actually ends. It only ends once you have permanently retired from the workforce. The best example of this, a person who took a shoe box and every time they interacted with someone that helped them along their journey, they would sit down and write them a quick thank you note and put it into their shoe box. Once they landed their next opportunity they took the shoe box to the post office and mailed all of the thank you notes out to the people that had helped them along their journey. There is nothing like receiving a personalized note from someone you had helped knowing they remembered and appreciated your support. If you need help in the future they will remember you. These practices will increase the agility of your network.

Once everything is said and done, it is necessary to go through the reflection process on what worked well and what did not.

Were your Landing Zone Areas properly defined and if not, what was missing? If training or certifications were missing it is best to get a current training plan started right away while you are working in your new position over the next 20 to 36 months. Often times these items are discovered during the interviewing process. How did your network respond to you when you reached out to them? If they jumped into immediate action then your network is healthy. If not, it may mean that you are going to have to spend extra effort in personal time interacting with your network. You can get the first interaction for help easier than the second if you are not investing in the relationships of your network. You want to make sure that you are not perceived as they are only contacting me when they need something. Invest time in your network and you will be rewarded.

You get out as much if not more
of what you put into your network!

Chapter Eight

Negotiations, Acceptance, Two Week Notice, Quitting Gracefully

The number one thing during conditions and negotiations of a job offer is that once an agreement is made it is extremely important to get it in writing. No exceptions. If they call you on the phone and tell you the offer you can verbally say that you like the offer, but you would like to review it in writing. Have them email it to you or send it to you in the mail. You can send them back a formal written acceptance. The amount that they sometimes offer you in the beginning is what is called a low ball offer. It is imperative that you know what you are worth. This is where financial planning and having reserves allows you to hold your ground. You can now counter with the salary amount that you command. Your knowledge of the market information for a particular region, the salaries being paid for the position and additional skills that are a premium benefit to the company are now considered factors. An example of this would be someone with Black Belt in statistics in the industry makes approximately $10K more per year than someone in the same position without having the certification. Your research to know what you are worth now pays off.

Once you get the job offer in writing and have accepted it, wait before you notify your current employer of your resignation. Once you get the acceptance completed you still have to complete your back ground checks, drug testing (if required) and any other testing. Make 100% sure there are no issues before you resign from your existing employer.

There has been more than one occasion when a person tells their existing employer they are resigning only to find out they failed their entrance drug test screening, unpaid parking ticket with an arrest warrant outstanding, or they missed the court date for that unpaid parking ticket, an exceptionally poor credit rating or a pre-existing condition. Make 100% sure by getting a note from the hiring company that you are all good and clear before you send in your notice.

Once you resign from the company help them above and beyond if they need help from you transferring information or processes to help them in the transition of losing a critical resource. Put your best professional foot forward before departing. Often times you might get a phone call a couple of months later from them trying to figure out something that you used to do and you can step them through the process. It is crucial to never burn any bridges in your career since it will negatively affect your network agility. It takes a long time to build up a successful network and a remarkably short time to destroy it. Always, always be a professional by being courteous and kind when called upon for assistance, regardless of the situation.

Chapter Nine

Consulting / 1099 / W2 / All in.

If you are an impacted person from a senior level position and have the ability to perform consulting work you should seriously consider this option. Consulting increases your chances of a faster transition, not to mention it is an excellent way to build out your network and meet extraordinarily high level people in other companies. Sometimes after being in a single company for a unusually long time, many people like the change of pace that consulting brings with the varying projects and increased travel.

If you want to see the world, become a consultant.

Most long term people do not know how to integrate into a consulting role, company or lifestyle. This determination is the hardest to collaborate, but a must for your landing zone management and planning. If you have a lot of experience in a certain area, it often can be utilized by other companies. Six Sigma, Operational Excellence, Human Resources, Supply Chain management, Logistics and Enterprise Tools like Oracle, SAP, SAS are some examples of cross industry functions. Remember that just because you have the skills does not mean it is a 100% shoe in. That is why doing your research upfront will allow you to understand and how to prepare to be covered with the time you need from your landing zone evaluations and planning.

There is an ultra-high probability with more companies moving to using more contract labor forces that you might be forced into consulting at some point in your career, so it is extremely valuable to prepare for it now. Being a consultant means you might not always get a steady paycheck. In some cases you will not get paid until the company gets paid from the customer receiving the consulting services. Being able to budget your finances is particularly critical, so ensure you can cover your expenses for the float between the time you give your services and the time you get paid. Most of the pain for a consultant is covering the travel expenses and how are they billed to the client. The way to resolve this issue is to ask for a flat rate per day added onto the consulting charges. So if you are charging $1500 per day for consulting services you could add on a Flat rate of $500 per day for all travel expenses if services are longer than two days. For example if you were teaching a Six Sigma Class for four days you would charge your client a flat rate of $8000. It might seem like a lot, but the companies are receiving the services across multiple people and they do not have to deal with monitoring the travel receipts and transaction accounting costs.

The difference between a 1099 and W2 is extremely large and this is the single most noteworthy thing to understand when you are going to engage consulting. For the 1099, the company is going to pay you a flat rate per hour of services. They are going to file a 1099 form and you are expected to pay your taxes from the funds that they paid you. A W2 means the company is going to pay you and take out a certain percentage of taxes for you. If you are a 1099 person, make sure you save the appropriate funds to ensure you can cover the taxes you owe at the end of the year. The best practice if you are consulting is to send in your required tax money owed to the IRS quarterly, so you do not get to the end of the year with an enormous tax bill.

When you first get contacted by a consulting firm or recruiter they are going to ask you what your "all in" number is going to be for your services. If you do not know what the number is, I suggest you figure it out ahead of time so when they ask you, you can tell them and explain the number to them so they understand it. If you do not have an all in number the recruiter will know you are not a consultant and skip over you for the opportunity.

The all in number is the total number per hour for salary, insurance, travel expenses, retirement savings / investments, and to pay your own taxes.

Now remember your all in number is not going to be paid to you weekly, but only on the hours you are going to be actually doing consulting work or services. If you know the number you need to make for your salary per year, add to that your estimated travel expenses and then mark up the entire amount by 30% for taxes and then divide that total number by the total hours of estimated work for the entire year since it is not going to 2080 hours. If your total rollup is $150K per year and you are only going to be working six months out of the year, your all in number would be around $150 per hour, not including travel expenses. If you misquoted your all in number you might create yourself a problem, but often it takes one time going through the consulting process being burned to actually learn how it works for the second go around.

The best time to calculate your all in number is prior to getting the call about the opportunity from the recruiter. Knowing what you are worth and what you are going to charge for your services ahead of time, will save you a lot of heart ache of missing a great opportunity when it comes to you unexpectedly.

Chapter Ten

Innovation, Companies and the New Mobile Workforce

The days of the employee being the number one asset of a company are gone. It is in the best interest of the company to have employees feeling like they are a family joined together as a startup. This quickly changes, especially if a startup is looking to go public.

With the new mobile workforce model of continuous churn will not allow employees to feel like they are stake holders and entrepreneurs (Owners) of the company, which is the number one key ingredient to develop a successful company. If employees think and feel they own the company growth is inevitable. If employees never reach total fulfillment they will never reach their innovation potential and in the long-term companies will miss their innovation periods unable to maintain competitiveness in the market.

Companies are counting on the Mobile Workforce for creating their current and future innovations. Companies compensate them well. In order to keep their edge they can only innovate to a certain level. They will always have to hold a little back for the next opportunity.

The Mobile Workforce will never achieve total fulfillment with job security and the company is not able to reach their highest innovation potential.

From a competitive position the IP (Intellectual Property) of a company is held within its individual resources. You are competing against resources. Get the critical resources and you get all of the keys to the kingdom! The key resources are not fresh outs, but the ones working for competing companies. Companies have segmented down the systems into individual parts to limit the IP loss from occurring. Since the entire system is limited in view, it limits innovation on the entire system level. This leaves innovation of only the sub parts of the system. Giving too large of an area of responsibility, you will lose possible IP when they leave or too little and perhaps they are not able to innovate disruptive products that are compelling in the market place.

Without a loyal workforce you are always going to have long-term sustainability issues. Granted you can pay for loyalty up to a certain point, but there is always another suitor waiting in the wings for the opportunity to get in the game. Part of the Landing Zone value determination of an individual is to understand the value of the IP you own and what you create for a company.

Any company that thinks they are going to create all of their innovation by attracting all of the best talent straight out of school is going to be disappointed short and long-term. This is the paradoxical situation for a company. Without a loyal workforce reaching total fulfillment the innovation process will never reach its maximum potential, and the company long term will not have sustainability. As an unintended consequence margins will erode and growth will perish.

A good example of this is if you are creating a lot of innovations that have no real practical value to a sustainable ecosystem. This is what I call the NOW innovation. It is innovation created to serve the immediate needs without a long-term vision or roadmap. It is as if following a path that is constantly being molded around the NOW requirements. An innovation that is too early for the market place is a wasted innovation.

You cannot innovate for the sake of innovation. The innovation process in this case is very costly, short lived and cannot be sustain. Innovation from the individual is internally driven to achieve stability and sustainably for themselves... The company benefits indirectly. Sustainability of the company is determined by its individuals driving for security and fulfillment for themselves by innovating. Once the company is no longer sustainable, innovation will perish and as an unintended consequence so will the company. When this happens other companies look to purchase the company for the rights to the intellectual property without the intention of keeping the business running or with the intention to sell the business off right away to another suitor. The intellectual property is then combined into other products or assigned to the highest bidder.

Companies have to go out and acquire other companies in order to survive. Long term they will not be able to stay in front of the fast followers and will eventually be replaced as their core values as a company will not be able to extend their existence, and they will disappear.

Think back to some of the all-time leading companies and you will see this sustainability of innovation pattern. Look at the current high tech companies and you will recognize leading technology developed without a long-term strategy. "Great we got it to work! "Now, what do we do with it? "How is this going to generate revenues for the company again?"

Today's companies that have been successful are the fast followers with value added innovation on top of existing concepts. Short-term incremental feature improvements are missing the long-term disruption product creation plans which create new markets. These markets are needed to reach the next level in creating an ecosystem of value by decreasing complexity and increasing utility. Most of this occurs through innovation that often starts out with the desire of the end in mind or making life simpler. Determining what are the needs and not just delivering particular solutions to a problem in the form of a product is the key to the future.

All innovation starts from within an individual's personal desire to create. The most important thing to remember is that you are that person!

Summary

Once you have gone through the entire process, whether it is the first time or the one hundredth time. There are some key life lessons to make sure you always keep close to your heart.

- *Your work does not define who you are.*

- *Love yourself; know yourself, and your self-worth.*

- *Always be prepared financially, mentally and physically.*

- *Continually improve your skills to maintain competitiveness. Spend an hour every day to learn something new that you did not know previously.*

- *You are working for the benefit of yourself, your family and no one else.*

- *You are responsible for everything that happens to you, accept it responsibly.*

- *Visualize the Career that you want! Write it down and work towards it every day.*

- *Money is only a means to get you to where you need to be; the real wealth comes to any individual through service and helping of others.*

- *The goal is to work so at some point you do not have to work. Start with the end in mind.*

- *Be thankful for all of the people who help you along the way and give back in as many ways as you can to other people who are experiencing what you have already experienced.*

- *Be kind and thankful to everyone and everything in your life, it does make a difference.*

- *Believe you can create or be part of something bigger than yourself.*

- *Be courageous with your thoughts and actions.*

- *Learn to listen; you might learn something you did not know.*

- *Never give up on yourself, in time it will happen.*

- *Indirect consequences are not part of the plan but part of the outcome, learn to see them from the beginning.*

- *Inventions can be bought but Innovation can only occur through understanding people's empathy.*

Special Appendix Section
Alternative 401K Investment IDEAS

This book in no way offers any financial or any other investing advice or recommendations to invest in anyway. In the event that you use any information in this book it is your constitutional right, the author and the publisher assume no responsibility for your actions.

There are many ways to self-fund for retirement. One of the key benefits of being let go from a company is that you can move the money out of your 401K into a traditional IRA account. If you were a long term employee and had taken advantage of the company 401k match and profit sharing plan over many years, this could have grown into a very substantial amount of money.

Most companies have a vested interest in keeping your money in their retirement account to help them with funding their current obligations taking benefits from their pension and retirement funds. My view is that when I go I take my finances with me! This allows more investing control of being able to get into and out of investments without having to wait for the market to close at the end of the trading day.

When you first start in the workforce your focus should not be to climb the corporate ladder but on how to become financially independent. In turn climbing the corporate ladder is a means to get there by consistently making more money over time, but it is not the only way. Learn how to balance your finances with the (cash equation) money coming in cannot be less than money going out. Make sensible spending decisions. For example, you do not have to buy a new car every three years. As long as it runs well, drive it. These types of savings will go a very long way over time.

There are many companies that manage self-directed IRA's that allow you to make alternative investments other than stocks or bonds. Here is a link to an example of one of those companies where you can research different types of retirement assets and alternate investments. http://tinyurl.com/pk4832s

After working for a company many years the probability of earning less than you did previously is much higher if you are reentering the workforce after losing your previous employment at the same type of position. After many salary increases for inflation year after year from your previous position it could have raised your salary very high but when you lose your employment you are back to where you started from. You would not want this decrease in pay adjustment to impact your lifestyle. Often times the reentry point to the workforce causes a drop in pay which forces you to stop funding your 401K or IRA. You still want to fund for your retirement or create consistent future income.

If you want to a way to self-fund your IRA with a year after year income, granted it would be a much lower CAP rate than you could get in stocks but it would be more evenly consistent investment is in alternative assets.

Most people do not know you can buy alternative assets with your traditional IRA. As an example, a person took a landing zone position at a company that made 30% less than at their previous position. Using one of the self-directed IRA companies, they took 50% of their transferred 401K money to an IRA and invested it into a real estate investment outright that rented in total for $3,100 a month. This rent after expenses, all goes back into the self-directed IRA trust account. Total taxes, insurance, maintenance and fees run about $12,200 a year, thus giving them a $25,000 positive cash flow into their retirement account. This buys them the option in their current position to decide to only do the company 401k match if offered or to not put any money away for retirement out of their paycheck since it is already being self-funded through the other investment.

By not having to fund for your retirement it is like getting a raise or being able to afford the same lifestyle with less money.

This investment strategy is harder if you have to get the other financing from a bank but it shows the basic concept of different ideas to fund your retirement other than coming from your paycheck.

At any time with these alternative investments they can be sold and moved back into traditional IRA investments if desired. These types of alternative investments take much longer to sell, requires fees to manage them and there is no guarantee of making money, it is like everything else in the investing world, proceed at your own risk and understanding.

CAUTION! Believe it or not there are people that prey on those who are unemployed to try to tap into their retirement savings, so be very careful with investment advice. If something seems too good to be true, it probably is! When in doubt move slowly. Ask advice from wealthy people you already know on what to do and what they think about your investment plans. They will help you if you ask them for advice on investment ideas.

This book in no way offers any financial or any other investing advice or recommendations to invest in anyway. In the event that you use any information in this book it is your constitutional right, the author and the publisher assume no responsibility for your actions.

Landing Zone Plan Worksheet

Top Locations I would like to reside at:
1)
2)
3)
4)
5)

Top Companies / Industries I would like to work in:
1)
2)
3)
4)
5)

Skills required for working at each Company/Industry:
1)
2)
3)
4)
5)

Top Network Contact at each Company / Industry:
1)
2)
3)
4)
5)

CONTACT NOTES

Top Contact at Locations I would like to reside at:
1)
2)
3)
4)
5)

Top Contacts at Target Companies / Industries:
1)
2)
3)
4)
5)

Top Networking Groups for Target Company/Industry:
1)
2)
3)
4)
5)

Networking Meeting Schedule and locations:
1)
2)
3)
4)
5)

CONTACT NOTES

_____
1)
2)
3)
4)
5)

_____
1)
2)
3)
4)
5)

_____
1)
2)
3)
4)
5)

_____
1)
2)
3)
4)
5)

FOLLOW-UP NOTE REMINDERS

Networking Meeting Introductions:
1)
2)
3)
4)
5)

Interviewers:
1)
2)
3)
4)
5)

Coincidental Introductions:
1)
2)
3)
4)
5)

Introductions from Friends:
1)
2)
3)
4)
5)

Appendix

Hiring Manager Target

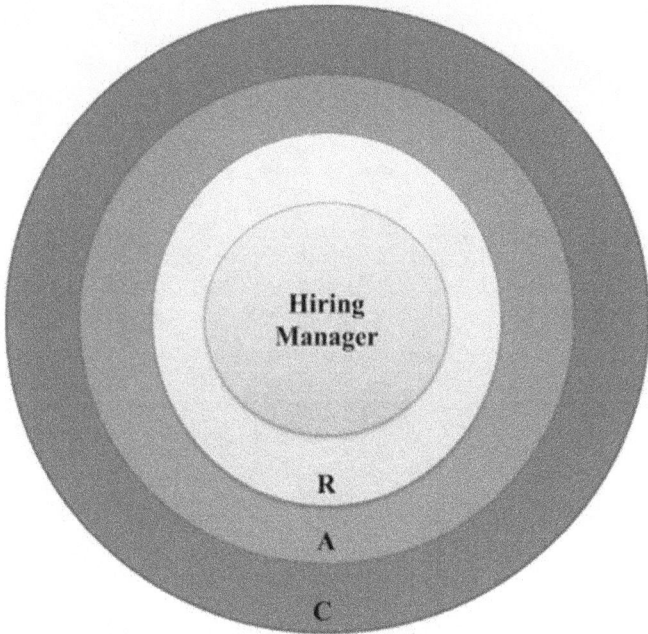

C = Contacts Aware of an Opportunity

A = People Aware of an Opportunity

R = Runner to the Hiring Manager

Map Out Your Connection Network by Contact and Company

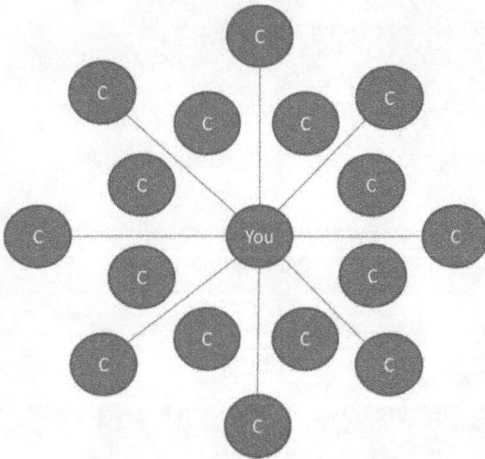

Largest Networked Contacts

Top Network Contact with Largest Networks Contacts
1)
2)
3)
4)
5)

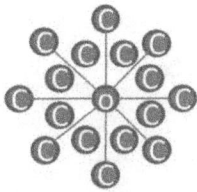

Contacts → Aware of an Opportunity

Aware = People Aware of an Opportunity

Runner → Hiring Manager

The Runner leads you to the Hiring Manager

"**C.A.R.**" (C → A → R)

Contacts Aware Runner

Drive your **C.A.R.** to your next Destination!

RUNNER NOTES

_____

1)
2)
3)
4)
5)

_____

1)
2)
3)
4)
5)

_____

1)
2)
3)
4)
5)

_____

1)
2)
3)
4)
5)

Typical Screening Questions

Employer:
Preferred Location or Location:
Employment Dates:
Education History:
Certifications:
Skills:
Work Summary:
Security Clearance:
Base Salary:
Stock Options:
Bonus:
Total Comp Package Required:
Interview Availability:
Available Start Date:
PTO Requirement Estimates:
Work Eligibility Status:
Updated Passport:
Availability for Drug Test Screening:

Tell me about yourself? (Not a repeat of your resume)

What was the reason you left your last position?

Why are you here and why should we hire you?

Why this position? Why now? (Why, Why, Why)

Why would a person as talented as you want to work for a company like this?

If you are so talented why did you stay at the same company for so long?

How do you explain your gap in employment?

Why this company, what do we do that interests you?

What is your definition of leadership?

In order to make change happen in an organization what is the first thing that must occur?

Do you have any special skillsets, talents or certifications?

If you were thinking on changing something how would you approach it?

Do you believe in asking for forgiveness rather than permission, or are you inclined to be sure your manager are in full agreement before you act?

What do you do when you are stressed out? What sorts of things irritate you the most or get you overly excited agitated or down and depressed?

What are your personal developmental needs and what are your plans to deal with them?

What have been the most difficult criticisms of your previous work? How did you handle them?

How would you describe your sense of humor?

What motivates you and demotivates you?

In terms of your career, where do you want to be in 1, 3, 5 years?

If you could have the perfect day, what would it consist of?

Would your references and current manager consider you an "A" or "B" player? Why?

What will your references describe as your strongest and weakest points?

Describe a complex situation that describes your leadership skills?

What are a couple of the most difficult or challenging decisions you have made?

What thought methodologies did you use to make the decisions and how did you make those decisions?

What are the principles do you live by?

In the last company you worked for did you feel like an employee or more of an owner of the company and why?

What are the best examples of your creativity in processes, systems, methods, products, structure, or services?

In the past year, what specifically have you done in order to remain knowledgeable about your field or in your industry?

What are the biggest risks you have taken in recent years? Include ones that have worked out well and not so well.

If you found a $50 bill on the floor at work or on the street; what would you do with it and why?

How have you borrowed, created, or applied best practices? If so how?

Describe a situation in which the pressures to compromise your integrity was the strongest. What did you do?

What sorts of obstacles have you faced in your most recent or current job?

What are examples of circumstances in which you were expected to do something on your own and you went beyond the call of duty?

What would you consider yourself obsessive about something and what would it be?

INTERVIEW QUESTION NOTES

_____

1)
2)
3)
4)
5)

_____

1)
2)
3)
4)
5)

_____

1)
2)
3)
4)
5)

_____

1)
2)
3)
4)
5)

INTERVIEW QUESTION NOTES

_____

1)
2)
3)
4)
5)

_____

1)
2)
3)
4)
5)

_____

1)
2)
3)
4)
5)

_____

1)
2)
3)
4)
5)

PERSONAL NOTES

1)
2)
3)
4)
5)

1)
2)
3)
4)
5)

1)
2)
3)
4)
5)

1)
2)
3)
4)
5)

www.ingramcontent.com/pod-product-compliance
Lightning Source LLC
La Vergne TN
LVHW091206080426
835509LV00006B/850